GET YOUR

DEATH

IN ORDER

Preparing Your
Heart and Your House

So Nothing Is Left Undone

B. FAYE ANDERSON, ESQ

ANCHORED LIFE® PUBLISHING

9212 Fry Rd., Ste 105, Box 363, Cypress, TX 77433

This book and all other Anchored Life Publishing books are available at bookstores and distributors worldwide.

Reach us on the Internet:
www.anchoredlifepublishing.com

ISBN 979-8-9940971-0-6

ISBN eBook: 979-8-9940971-1-3

ISBN Audiobook: 979-8-9940971-2-0

For Worldwide Distribution, Printed in the U.S.A.

Disclaimer

This book is intended for general informational and educational purposes only. It is not a substitute for legal or financial advice. Although the author is a licensed attorney, reading this book does not create an attorney–client relationship. Laws vary by state and circumstances; readers should consult a qualified attorney regarding their individual situations.

The information contained herein reflects general principles of estate planning and faith-based stewardship as of the time of publication and may not apply to specific cases. The author and publisher disclaim any liability arising from actions taken or not taken based on the contents of this book.

Dedication

For my father,

You proved that it's not how you start, but how you finish.

Even in your passing, I learned things I never knew; stories that spoke of resilience, kindness, and a love that ran deep.

You didn't have an easy life, but your mission became clear:
to make life easier for the people you loved.

Though you weren't always protected, you made it your legacy to protect others.

Though you couldn't always be present, when it mattered you showed up.

You left this world knowing Christ,
with your death in order and your legacy intact.

You were one of those rare souls who didn't just pass through life;
you left an impression.

I honor your life, your love, and your finish.

Acknowledgments

To my husband: Thank you for being my steady place, my calm in the storm, and the one who reminds me I don't have to carry everything alone. Your love has anchored me in more ways than I can count.

To my sons: Thank you for giving me purpose beyond the pages. You are the reason I think about legacy, the reason I press forward with intention, and the reason I want to leave this world better than I found it.

To my mother: Your wisdom, prayers, and unconditional love have been a covering over my life. You've shown me what it means to be faithful, even when life doesn't go as planned.

To every person who picks up this book, thank you for doing the hard but needed work of preparing for the end while living fully in the now. My prayer is that this helps you walk in peace, with purpose, with nothing left undone.

Preface

I didn't write this book because I'm obsessed with death. I wrote it because I'm committed to peace—yours and your family's.

We spend years planning weddings, buying homes, building careers, and saving for retirement; yet many never prepare for the one appointment we're guaranteed to keep: the day we leave this earth.

Our culture avoids death until it barges through the front door. Grieving families are left to scramble, make uninformed decisions, and worry whether they're honoring their loved one's wishes. Far too often, I have witnessed confusion, conflict, and raw emotional pain. Sometimes there's a life insurance policy that leaves money but does not necessarily leave peace. Leaving your financial affairs in disarray is one thing, but leaving this world with your spiritual house in chaos is even more tragic. Every time I encounter such a situation, my heart breaks for the grieving families.

This book is not just about paperwork, financial tidiness, or legal preparation. It's about worship, fiscal intentionality, and spiritual stewardship. It's about getting your house in order, both secularly and spiritually. It's about knowing where you'll spend eternity so that when your time comes, you can hear, *"Well done, my good and faithful servant..."* (Matthew 25:21 NLT). It's about leaving a legacy that honors God and loves others well, both before and after your final breath.

Preparing for death is one of the most courageous, Christ-like acts you can undertake. Jesus didn't wait until death to declare His will. He expressed it daily—teaching, blessing, forgiving. From the cross, He even ensured His mother's care. Jesus modeled what it means to care for others and leave nothing undone. From the cross, amid unimaginable pain, He looked down and made sure His mother would be cared for:

> *"When Jesus saw his mother standing there beside the disciple he loved, he said to her, "Dear woman, here is your son." And he said to this disciple, "Here is your mother." And from then on this disciple took her into his home."*
> — *John 19:26–27 (NLT)*

This act wasn't just sentimental; it was intentional. Jesus was fulfilling His responsibility as a son, making sure His mother wouldn't be left alone. That moment is a powerful example of how love, legacy, and stewardship go hand in hand, even at death.

That's what this book is about: living and leaving in divine order. It's about aligning your life and your legacy with God's will. It's about preparing your heart and your house— so that nothing is left undone. Jesus showed us how to live with purpose and die with intention. We should do the same.

This isn't a fear-based journey; it's a faith-based invitation. Each chapter walks you through the process step by step— spiritually or practically. If you commit to the process, you'll gain something priceless: the peace that comes from knowing, "I have stewarded well. I've left nothing undone." Like Jesus, I want to leave nothing unresolved; spiritually or practically. As He declared in His final moments, *"It is finished"* (John 19:30 NLT).

Whether you're young or old, wealthy or not, saved or still seeking, this book is for you.

If you've delayed this conversation until now, grace means you still have time. It's not too late to get your house in order, both spiritually and practically.

Let's begin.

Table of Contents

Chapter 1: Facing the Truth

We Will All Die One Day

Legacy from Scripture

Moses knew his time was coming to an end.
Before he died, he climbed Mount Nebo to view the
Promised Land, blessed the tribes of Israel, gave final
instructions, and was gathered to God in peace
(Deuteronomy 32–34, NLT).
He faced death with clarity, not fear.
**His preparation ensured his people could move
forward without him.**

You don't need a terminal diagnosis to begin preparing for
death. You only need to accept a truth that many spend a
lifetime avoiding: your time on earth will come to an end,
and perhaps sooner than you expect.

As Scripture reminds us, *"How do you know what your
life will be like tomorrow? Your life is like the morning*

fog—it's here a little while, then it's gone." (James 4:14, NLT).

It sounds harsh, but the Word of God never promised immortality in this life. What is offered is something deeper: the courage to face reality and the wisdom to live well.

When Jesus said, *"And you will know the truth, and the truth will set you free"* (John 8:32, NLT), he wasn't speaking only about salvation from sin. He was revealing the liberating power of truth itself. Truth breaks spiritual, emotional, and generational chains. One of the most freeing truths you can embrace is the knowledge that your time on this Earth is limited.

When you deny death, you live like you have endless tomorrows. That illusion leads to spiritual apathy, financial disorder, and relational delay. But when you accept that it *"is destined to die once and after that comes judgment"* (Hebrews 9:27, NLT), everything shifts. You stop deferring purpose. You stop delaying obedience. You stop assuming your family will "just know what to do" when you are gone.

I had to confront this truth personally. My death isn't mine alone to experience. I have a wonderful husband and two handsomely gifted boys. My death will become a defining moment in the lives of everyone I love. How I prepare or fail to prepare for it will become part of their story too.

We prepare for everything else—school, weddings, careers, retirement, but we often ignore the one event guaranteed for every soul: death.

This isn't morbid; it's merciful. It's not about death; it's about how you live and what you leave behind.

Ecclesiastes reminds us there's *"a time to be born and a time to die"* (Ecclesiastes 3:2, NLT). Don't think of death as interruption, because it's not. Death is an appointment, written into life's rhythm by the same God who wrote your beginning.

When we approach death with faith instead of fear, we see it not as an end but as a continuation. Preparing spiritually and practically is not morbid; it's faithful, obedient, and loving.

Reading this book is not grim; it's wise. *"Getting wisdom is the wisest thing you can do! And whatever else you do, develop good judgment"* (Proverbs 4:7, NLT). You are choosing clarity over confusion, peace over panic, and truth over illusion.

When Psalm 90:12 (NLT) says, *"Teach us to realize the brevity of life, so that we may grow in wisdom,"* it's not calling us to a state of anxiety. It's a call to intentionality. To number your days is to treat each one as sacred; lived not in fear, but in purpose.

But let's go deeper.

Organizing your earthly affairs is important, but it means little if your eternal destiny remains unsettled. Jesus asked, *"And what do you benefit if you gain the whole world but lose your own soul?"* (Mark 8:36, NLT). You could leave behind a perfectly ordered estate and still face eternity separated from God.

That's not order; that's a tragedy.

So before we continue, let me ask: If your heart stopped today, would your soul be at peace with God?

If you're unsure, this is your moment. Not to fear death, but to face it through the lens of the cross. Jesus died and rose again to give you eternal life. Not just peace on earth, but a home in heaven.

"There is more than enough room in my Father's home. If this were not so, would I have told you that I am going to prepare a place for you?" (John 14:2, NLT). His arms are open—not to condemn you, but to receive you.

If you're ready, pray this prayer out loud:

> "Lord Jesus, I believe You are the Son of God. I believe You died for my sins and rose from the grave. Please forgive me. I surrender my heart and life to You. Lead me from this day forward. Be my Savior, my Lord, and my peace. In Jesus' name, Amen."

That prayer isn't a ritual; it's a doorway. If you prayed that prayer, welcome into the body of Christ. You've taken the most important step in getting your death in order, ensuring your name is written in the Book of Life.

Now let's turn to the practical. Honoring God includes stewarding what He's entrusted to you.

We've faced the truth; now we begin the preparation. Not just any preparation—peace-making preparation rooted in faith, love, and wisdom.

And the first tool we need isn't legal; it's a mindset.

Estate planning isn't about how much you have; it's about how you care for the people you leave behind.

That applies to everyone, not just the wealthy.

Whether you rent or own, whether you live paycheck to paycheck or have multiple accounts, you still have:

- Decisions that must be made.
- People you care about.
- A story you want to tell, even after you're gone.

Think of estate planning as the natural counterpart to your spiritual testimony. It tells the story of what mattered to you, how you provided, and how you stewarded God's gifts.

Ask yourself:

- If I died today, who would manage what I leave behind?

- Who would receive my possessions, accounts, or unfinished business?
- Who would care for my children if they're minors?
- How would my debts be handled?
- Would my loved ones know what I wanted spiritually, financially, and practically?
- Do they even know where to find my important documents?

If you're unsure, you're not alone; but you are in the right place.

Facing death isn't just a legal task; it's a discipleship moment.

Here are two real-life stories:

Denise's father was godly and kind but left no will. Denise grieved not only the loss of her father but also the burden of guessing at his wishes and navigating probate court. Instead of simply mourning, she found herself answering questions from attorneys, going through and gathering family records, attending hearings, and facing creditors. She even worried about whether the mortgage could be paid before the property was lost. A beautiful life ended in confusion, and the lack of direction became a grief of its own.

Victor had modest means but clear plans: a simple will, named accounts, and a letter to his children about his faith. Because of that preparation, his family was able to grieve together without confusion. Instead of scrambling for documents or struggling with creditors, they were guided by his clarity. His planning became part of his testimony, leaving his family peace along with their memories. His preparation became a gift to those he loved.

The difference? Not wealth, wisdom.

Think of it like Noah building the ark. He didn't wait for the storm; he prepared in peace. Estate planning is your ark. You don't build it in a crisis; you build it in calmness.

Legacy in Real Life

Angela was 38 when her mother passed away suddenly. No warning. No plans. What followed were weeks of stress, fighting among siblings, and financial scrambling. Angela cried as she signed the cremation papers, unsure if it was what her mother even wanted. She told me, "No one should have to guess in grief. That's why I'm getting my house in order."

Reflection & Application

Facing the truth gives us the power to prepare with faith and peace. Ask yourself the following questions, and take time to reflect honestly and prayerfully.

- What have I been avoiding?
    - Have I ignored conversations about death or delayed important decisions?
- Have I prayed about this?
    - Have I invited God into the planning?
    - Have I trusted Him to guide me in both spiritual and practical steps?
- Would my family know what to do if I died today?
    - Would they know what I believed?
    - Would they find order or disarray?
- What's one small step I can take this week?

Now take a step forward. Small actions can make an eternal difference.

- Write your testimony.
- Write down your assets.
- Begin a conversation with your family about your wishes.

- Schedule an appointment with an estate planning attorney.

Declare this over yourself:

> "I face the truth with faith, not fear. I am a steward of my soul and household. I've surrendered to Christ and am walking in peace. I will not leave confusion behind. I will leave a legacy of wisdom, clarity, and eternal hope."

End of Chapter Summary

Spiritual Principles

- **John 8:32** – Truth frees us from fear, denial, and avoidance.
- **Ecclesiastes 3:2** – Death is appointed, not accidental.
- **Hebrews 9:27** – Acknowledging mortality prepares us for eternity.
- **Proverbs 4:7** – Seeking wisdom is faithful stewardship.
- **Psalm 90:12** – Life's brevity calls us to intentional living.

Theological Insight

Truth brings clarity, and clarity gives peace. The gospel invites us not only to eternal life but to live wisely in light of death. When we stop avoiding the truth, we start living and leaving in order.

Chapter 2: In My Will: Living and Leaving According to Divine Order

Understanding Wills, Heirs, and Inheritance

Legacy from Scripture

Jacob gathered his sons and spoke final blessings over each one before he died (Genesis 49). He not only spoke prophetically, but he also gave burial instructions that his sons honored.

He left a legacy that shaped the future of a nation.

One of the most dangerous assumptions we make spiritually and practically is, *"They'll know what to do,"* or *"They'll know what I would have wanted."* But intention without instruction breeds confusion. Whether in matters of faith or finances, assumption is not stewardship. Assumption is not legacy.

God doesn't operate in assumption; He operates in clarity.

From Genesis to Revelation, God speaks specifically. He calls His children by name. He makes covenants. He assigns inheritance with precision. Our Heavenly Father doesn't leave His promises up for interpretation; He documents them. He seals them with blood. He makes it clear who belongs to Him and what He has promised them.

"And since we are his children, we are his heirs. In fact, together with Christ we are heirs of God's glory" (Romans 8:17, NLT). That's not a poetic metaphor; it's a spiritual legal truth. If you belong to God, you inherit what He has prepared. But inheritance must be named. That's true in heaven, and it's true on earth.

In the Kingdom of God, only those *in Christ* inherit eternal life. Likewise, in your earthly estate, only those *named* inherit what you leave behind.

Some people assume their loved ones (spouse, children, or parents) will automatically inherit everything. They say, *"Everyone knows who my family is."* But in reality, without a will, even direct descendants must go to court and *prove* their relationship. They're left to navigate a burdensome and uncertain process.

The same is true spiritually. If your name isn't written in the Lamb's Book of Life, you will not enter heaven. At the end of the day—whether it's written in God's book, in a legal will, or in a court order—what's written is what stands.

There's a deeper lesson here: being *in His will* isn't just about living rightly, it's about being written into God's divine legacy. And just as you want to be included in His will, your loved ones need to be included in yours.

That means you can't leave your legacy to chance. You must name your heirs. You must write it down. You must plan with intention, prayer, and clarity.

Imagine this scene: A family gathers in court after a loved one's passing, hoping to hear their names read aloud. The attorney opens the will, and their names aren't there—not because they weren't loved, but because they weren't named.

Now picture another moment: the Book of Life is opened. You want your name in it not because you lived perfectly, but because you accepted Christ, who wrote you in.

God doesn't deal in assumption, and neither should we.

Jesus said, *"For I have come down from heaven to do the will of God who sent me, not to do my own will"* (John 6:38, NLT). Even the Son of God submitted to divine order. He didn't live by preference; He lived by assignment. And through that obedience, He secured the greatest inheritance of all: salvation for those who believe.

"I take joy in doing your will, my God, for your instructions are written on my heart" (Psalm 40:8, NLT). God's will is not a burden: it's a joy. Obedience brings alignment. Alignment brings clarity. And clarity brings peace.

If we delight to walk in God's will, we should also find purpose in putting our earthly will in order. This isn't just about legal preparations; it's sacred stewardship. A Last Will and Testament serves both a legal and spiritual purpose. A will is a written declaration of stewardship, love, and clarity. Just as God names His heirs, we must name ours.

Planning your will is not about control; it's about care. It's not about materialism; it's about love.

To neglect this isn't humility, it's irresponsibility. Love prepares.

What Is a Will?

A Last Will and Testament is a legal document that:

- Details how you want your property and assets distributed;
- Names who receives what;
- Appoints a trusted person (executor) to carry out your wishes;
- Assigns guardianship for minor children (if applicable); and
- Helps avoid unnecessary court battles and confusion.

Who Needs a Will?

You do. Not because you're old. Not because you're wealthy. But because you're alive, and God has entrusted something to your care.

Good stewardship is never about how much you have; it's about how faithful you are in managing it.

You may not have much, but your will still matters. Why? Because your will is your voice when you can no longer speak. It tells your story, reflects your faith, and provides direction.

What Is an Executor?

An executor is someone you trust to carry out your instructions. They:

- Locate and gather your assets;
- Pay any final debts or taxes; and
- Distribute your property as outlined in your will.

Choose someone with integrity, discernment, and strength—not just someone close, but someone capable.

What Happens If You Die Without a Will?

Dying without a will is called *intestacy*. When this happens:

- The state decides who inherits your assets;
- A court appoints someone to manage your estate;
- Loved ones outside legal definitions (like stepchildren or close friends) may be excluded;
- Minor children's guardianship is decided by a judge; and
- Family tensions and legal delays often follow.

Each state has its own intestacy laws, so the outcome may not reflect your wishes. Without your voice, the system decides.

Dying without a will doesn't just leave legal confusion; it creates emotional wounds that could have been avoided.

Legacy in Real Life

Mr. Jefferson had three adult children and no will. He always said, *"They'll figure it out."* When he died, they didn't just *"figure it out."* They fought in court for 18 months. Relationships were broken, and the estate was nearly drained in legal fees. One daughter later said, *"I wish we had something written. That could have saved our family."*

Reflection & Application

If walking in God's will brings peace, then preparing your earthly will should reflect that same purpose and clarity. Ask yourself the following questions, and take time to reflect honestly and prayerfully.

- Am I confident that I'm living in God's will spiritually?
- Have I aligned my earthly affairs with that same intentionality?
- Have I named my loved ones or left them in a place of uncertainty?

- Beyond possessions, what values do I want to leave behind?

Now take a step forward. Small actions can make an eternal difference.

- List your intended heirs.
- Choose your executor.
- Attend your appointment with the estate planning attorney to begin your will.

Don't wait to finish everything. Just start.

Declare this over yourself:

> "I walk in the will of God and leave a legacy of order, peace, and provision. I live by assignment, not assumption. I leave behind clarity, not confusion."

End of Chapter Summary

Spiritual Principles

- **Romans 8:17** – Only God's children are named as heirs. So too, only named heirs receive earthly inheritance.

- **John 6:38** – Jesus submitted to divine order. Our lives and legacies should reflect the same.
- **Psalm 40:8** – Obedience to God's will reflects joy, not burden.
- **1 Corinthians 14:40** – Order is not optional; it is the mark of faithful stewardship.

Theological Insights

- God names and appoints with clarity; so should we.
- Heaven does not operate on guesswork; neither should your estate.
- A written will is more than legal; it is theological.
- Inclusion requires intention. Just as the Book of Life records names, so should your will.

God's will is the safest place to live from. Just as He includes us in His plan through grace, we are called to include our loved ones in our plan through love.

Chapter 3: Don't Leave the Bill Behind

Preneed Planning and Burial Insurance Made Simple

Legacy from Scripture

The widow in 2 Kings 4 was left with crushing debt after her husband died; so severe that the creditors threatened to enslave her sons. Elisha intervened, but the story shows what happens when financial burdens are left behind.

Love prepares. Debt can destroy.

Few conversations are harder than talking about death; except, perhaps, talking about how to pay for it.

But silence doesn't protect your family. It burdens them.

I've sat with grieving families torn between sorrow and a GoFundMe page. These were people who loved deeply but never imagined death would come so soon or cost so much. The average funeral in the U.S. ranges from $7,000 to $15,000. And when no plan is in place, families often face hard choices: maxing out credit cards, delaying services, or selling cherished possessions to cover the costs.

Failing to plan isn't just a financial oversight; it's a missed opportunity to steward your legacy in a way that honors God, cares for your loved ones, and reflects your faith.

"Good people leave an inheritance to their grandchildren" (Proverbs 13:22, NLT). That inheritance is not only financial; it's emotional. It's the peace of not having to decide everything under pressure. It's the mercy of preparation.

Jesus taught the wisdom of counting the cost:
 "But don't begin until you count the cost" (Luke 14:28, NLT). If we plan for weddings, college, and retirement, why not plan for our final departure?

The Apostle Paul said:
 "But those who won't care for their relatives, especially those in their own household, have denied the true faith. Such people are worse than unbelievers" (1 Timothy 5:8, NLT).

Providing for your family doesn't end at death; it includes what happens after.

This isn't morbid. It's mature.

Yes, your soul will be with the Lord, but your loved ones will still be here, navigating the details of your departure. In that sacred space between grief and logistics, your preparation can be a gift of love.

I've seen both sides:

- Families arguing over who pays for what;
- Children guessing at burial wishes; and
- Spouses overwhelmed by unexpected decisions.

And I've seen the peace that planning brings: wishes honored, expenses covered, and chaos replaced by calm.

Planning ahead isn't about money; it's about mercy. It says, "*I didn't just love you while I lived. I loved you enough to prepare for my death.*"

Let's look at the tools that make this easier. These options help ensure your final expenses are covered without leaving your family scrambling.

Preneed Funeral Plans

A preneed funeral plan is a written agreement with a funeral provider that allows you to make decisions and payments in advance.

- Burial or cremation
- Service details (e.g., casket, flowers, music, venue)
- Payment method (lump sum or installments)

Benefits:

- Locks in current prices (protecting against inflation);
- Clearly documents your wishes, avoiding guesswork; and
- Reduces emotional stress on your family during an already difficult time.

Considerations:

- May be non-transferable if you move or change providers; and
- Always verify the provider is licensed, insured, and reputable in your state.

Final Expense Insurance (Burial Insurance)

This is a small whole-life insurance policy ($5,000–$25,000) intended to cover funeral costs and other final expenses.

Benefits:

- Funds go directly to a named beneficiary, not the funeral home;
- Can be used for burial, travel, or unpaid bills; and
- Easy to qualify for; often no medical exam required.

Considerations:

- Premiums may add up over time; and
- Missed payments can cause the policy to lapse.

Payable-on-Death (POD) Bank Accounts

A POD account is a standard bank account that automatically transfers to a named beneficiary when you die, bypassing probate.

Benefits:

- Simplifies transfer of funds;
- Avoids probate delays; and

- Ensures assets go directly to your intended beneficiary.

Important Consideration:

While POD accounts offer faster access compared to probate, funds are not immediately available at the time of death. Most banks require a certified death certificate, which is typically issued after the funeral. Therefore, POD accounts should not be relied on for immediate funeral or emergency costs.

Traditional Life Insurance

Life insurance can cover final expenses, but the funds may take longer to access or be tied up in probate if there is no named beneficiary.

Tip: Don't rely on life insurance alone for immediate needs.

Comparison Summary

Tool	Covers	Who Receives Funds	Flexibility	Access Speed
Preneed Plan	Specific funeral details	Funeral provider	Low	Immediate
Burial Insurance	Any final expenses	Named beneficiary	High	24–72 hours
POD Account	Set-aside cash	Named person	High	Several weeks
Life Insurance	Broad financial needs	Policy beneficiary	Medium	Several weeks

Once you've made a plan, share it with your family.

Let them know:

- What you chose;
- Where your documents are stored; and
- Who to call and what to expect.

Don't let your departure leave your loved ones disoriented. Let it leave them grounded in peace, love, and clarity.

Tasha buried her aunt using a credit card. She never expected to pay $11,000 out of pocket for funeral costs, a casket, and burial.

> *"I would've said no," she admitted, "but I was her only niece, and I knew she'd want something nice."*

That experience changed her perspective. Today, Tasha pays $25 a month for a final expense insurance policy.

> *"That's my gift to my kids," she says. "I'll leave a plan, not a bill."*

Reflection & Application

Loving your family means planning ahead, so they're not left grieving with a bill in their hands. Ask yourself the following questions, and take time to reflect honestly and prayerfully.

- If I died today, who would pay for my funeral?
- Have I discussed my burial or memorial preferences with my family?

- Am I avoiding this conversation out of fear, or will I prepare in love?

Now take a step forward. Small actions can make an eternal difference.

- Review your existing insurance and bank accounts.
- Write down your burial or memorial preferences.
- Request quotes for pre-need plans and/or burial insurance.
- Choose a trusted person to share your plan with and have the conversation this week.

Declare this over yourself:

"My final act of stewardship will reflect my faith. I will prepare with mercy so my family can grieve in peace. I will not leave confusion. I will leave peace, provision, and clarity. My death will not bring chaos; it will reflect the order of my life and the faith of my heart."

End of Chapter Summary

Spiritual Principles

- **Proverbs 13:22** – A godly inheritance includes emotional and practical provision.
- **Luke 14:28** – Planning is spiritual wisdom, not guesswork.
- **1 Timothy 5:8** – Providing includes preparation beyond your final breath.

Theological Insights

- Death doesn't end your responsibility to love; it reveals it.
- Pre-planning is not only wise; it's worshipful.
- Stewardship extends to your last decision because our God is a God of order.

Grief is heavy enough. Don't add financial confusion to the weight your family must carry.

Planning your funeral in advance is not about wealth; it's about wisdom and love.

Chapter 4: When You Can't Speak for Yourself

Making Your Wishes Known

Legacy from Scripture

Jesus, in Gethsemane, expressed His wishes clearly: ***"Yet I want your will to be done, not mine"*** (Luke 22:42, NLT). Though facing death, He made His values known and surrendered to God's plan.

Even in silence, He had already spoken for Himself.

The Garden of Gethsemane was quiet, but it thundered with surrender.

There, beneath the weight of what was to come, Jesus prayed:

"Father, if you are willing, please take this cup of suffering away from me. Yet I want your will to be done, not mine" (Luke 22:42, NLT).

It wasn't just a moment of agony. It was a moment of trust.

You may never face what Jesus did. But you could face a moment (sudden or gradual) when you can no longer speak for yourself: a stroke, a coma, a critical illness. When that moment comes, someone will have to speak on your behalf.

The question is:
Will they know what to say, and will they have the authority to say it?

Advance planning for incapacity is not about control. It's about clarity. It's a gift— defense against confusion, emotional conflict, or legal chaos. It declares in wisdom and love: *"I trust God and I've made provision for what I cannot predict."*

Even Jesus entrusted His body and spirit to the Father: **"Father, I entrust my spirit into your hands"** (Luke 23:46, NLT). His surrender wasn't weakness; it was worship. He modeled what it means to plan with purpose and release with trust.

"We can make our plans, but the LORD determines our steps" (Proverbs 16:9, NLT). Planning does not mean we control outcomes. It means we serve those who may carry the weight when we no longer can.

The Holy Spirit is our eternal Advocate, interceding *"with groanings that cannot be expressed in words"* (Romans 8:26, NLT). But in the natural world, God gives us people (trusted agents) who can speak on our behalf when we no longer can.

That's where these tools come in.

There are two types of advance planning tools:

- **Healthcare tools** – for medical decisions
- **Financial tools** – for money and property

1. Living Will (Directive to Physicians)

A Living Will outlines your preferences for medical treatment if you are terminally ill or permanently unconscious and unable to communicate.

You can state:

- Whether you want life-sustaining treatment;
- Your preferences for artificial nutrition and hydration; and
- Whether you desire comfort care or pain relief only.

Why it matters:

If your values are written down, your loved ones won't have to guess or argue during a crisis.

2. Medical Power of Attorney (MPOA)

This document names someone (your agent) to make healthcare decisions for you when you're incapacitated.

Your agent can:

- Speak with doctors;
- Approve or decline treatments; and
- Access your medical records.

Choose someone who:

- Understands your values and faith;
- Can stay calm under pressure; and
- Will honor your wishes, not just their opinions.

Important: This agent only acts if you are unable to make decisions yourself.

3. HIPAA Authorization

This document allows specific individuals to access your private medical information. Without it, even a spouse or adult child may be denied access.

Include anyone you trust to be informed and involved in your care decisions.

4. Do Not Resuscitate Order (DNR)

A DNR instructs medical personnel not to perform CPR if your heart stops. This is typically used for those with terminal illness or who decline aggressive interventions.

A DNR is not part of your estate plan; it's a medical order that must be signed by a doctor. There are different forms for in-hospital and out-of-hospital use. Ask your provider about state-specific requirements.

5. Durable Power of Attorney (DPOA) – Financial

While your MPOA handles healthcare decisions, a Durable Power of Attorney gives someone legal authority to manage your finances if you become incapacitated.

Your financial agent can:

- Pay bills;
- Access bank accounts;
- Handle property or investments;
- File taxes; and
- Manage business affairs.

Note: Durable means it remains valid even if you become incapacitated, but it ends at death. After death, your executor (not your POA) takes over.

Who Needs These Documents?

You do, especially if you:

- Are over 18;
- Have children or dependents;
- Manage any money, property, or healthcare needs; or
- Want your values honored in a crisis.

These aren't just for the elderly. They're for the prepared.

How to Set Them Up

- Use free state-specific forms or consult an attorney;
- Sign with a notary or witnesses present as required;
- Store copies in a secure, accessible place;
- Share them with your agent(s) and loved ones; and

- Review them annually or after major life changes.

Legacy in Real Life

After a car accident, Marcus was in a coma for 11 days. He was only 42 and single. His father and mother disagreed about life support. Without a medical power of attorney or directive, the hospital had to keep him alive. He survived. And the first document he signed once home? A living will.

Reflection & Application

Silence doesn't mean you don't have a voice, unless you've left nothing in writing.

- If I couldn't speak, who would speak for me?
- Do I trust that person to follow my faith and values?
- Does that person know where my documents are?

Now take a step forward. Small actions can make an eternal difference.

- Choose your medical and financial agents;
- Complete a living will, MPOA, HIPAA release, and DPOA;
- Place copies in a secure location; and
- Inform your agents and key family members.

Declare this over yourself:

> "Even in silence, my life will speak. God is my
> advocate, and I have prepared in wisdom and
> peace. Those I trust will speak with love, clarity,
> and courage on my behalf. God is with me in
> every decision."

End of Chapter Summary

Spiritual Principles

- **Luke 22:42** – Obedience includes surrendering to
  God's will, even in suffering.
- **Proverbs 16:9** – We plan in humility, knowing God
  establishes our steps.
- **James 4:14–15** – Life is a mist. Preparation is
  wisdom, not fear.
- **Romans 8:26** – God intercedes when we cannot
  speak. So should our agents.
- **1 Corinthians 14:40** – Order honors God and
  protects our loved ones.
- **Proverbs 21:5** – Diligent plans lead to peace, not
  panic.

Theological Insights

- A medical or financial power of attorney is not a lifetime role; it's a temporary stewardship.
- You may lose your voice, but not your value. Advance planning ensures your values still speak.
- God prepares ahead. So should we.
- The Holy Spirit advocates spiritually; your appointed agents advocate naturally.

Planning for incapacity is not about control. It's about peace. Even Jesus spoke about what would happen to His body. We should do the same.

Chapter 5: The Business of Death

Organizing Finances and Leaving a Trail of Peace

Legacy from Scripture

Joseph, after saving Egypt through wise financial planning, made his family promise to carry his bones out of Egypt when the time came (Genesis 50:24–25, NLT). **He stewarded not only the present but gave direction for the future, even in death.**

When it comes to end-of-life preparation, **chaos is not compassion**. One of the most spiritual things you can do is get your financial affairs in order.

Scripture is clear: ***"But be sure that everything is done properly and in order"*** (1 Corinthians 14:40, NLT).

Death is not just a spiritual moment; it is also a financial event.

When someone passes, their accounts freeze. Their bills continue. And their loved ones are left trying to navigate a maze of paperwork, policies, and probate, often while grieving.

It's not just overwhelming. It's avoidable.

Jesus told the parable of the wise and foolish builders. One built on rock, the other on sand. The difference wasn't the storm; it was the preparation. Some prepare with clarity; others leave behind confusion.

And confusion comes with a cost: legal fees, delayed access to funds, strained relationships, and emotional exhaustion. Your silence now can become their storm later.

In Genesis 41, Joseph gave Pharaoh a divine strategy: save during the years of plenty to survive the years of famine. That preparation didn't just save Egypt; it preserved God's people.

That's the business of death: **putting order in place today so your loved ones can navigate tomorrow.**

This is not about fear; it's about faith.

Let's steward our financial lives with the same intentionality we give our spiritual ones: thoroughly, peacefully, and with love.

When you pass away, your loved ones will face dozens of financial decisions. You can make that process smoother or harder based on what you do now.

Here's how to prepare:

1. *Create a Financial Snapshot. List and organize all your key accounts and assets:*
   - Bank accounts (checking and savings)
   - Retirement accounts (401(k), IRA, pensions)
   - Life insurance policies
   - Property (mortgage, deeds, titles)
   - Vehicles
   - Credit cards and loans
   - Business interests
   - Digital assets (PayPal, Venmo, crypto, online platforms)

This is your **financial snapshot**, a map of everything you manage.

Tip: Store this list in one secure, accessible location. Use a locked cabinet, a password-protected digital file, or an encrypted cloud-based vault. And most importantly, make sure someone you trust knows how to access it.

2. Update Beneficiaries

Many financial assets bypass your will and transfer directly to the person named as your beneficiary. These include:

- Life insurance
- Retirement accounts
- Bank accounts with a Payable-on-Death (POD) designation

These designations override your will. If your ex-spouse is still listed as your life insurance beneficiary, they will receive the money even if your will says otherwise.

Review and update beneficiaries regularly, especially after major life changes.

3. Store and Share Key Documents

At minimum, make sure a trusted person knows how to access:

- Your will
- Your financial snapshot
- Insurance policies
- Digital account passwords or login instructions
- Contact info for your financial advisor or attorney

Don't just say, "It's in a folder somewhere." Walk someone through it.

Even a five-minute conversation can save them months of confusion.

4. Write a Letter of Instruction

Your will is legal. Your **letter of instruction** is personal.

Use this document to share practical details such as:

- How to access certain accounts;
- Where to find your safe deposit box key;
- Who to call for support or questions;
- Passwords, insurance policy numbers, or subscription accounts to cancel; and
- How to handle your business or household responsibilities in your absence.

Think of it as a love letter of logistics: one final act of kindness that reduces chaos.

5. Get Help

Don't wait for a crisis. If your financial life is messy or unclear, meet with:

- An estate planning attorney
- A financial advisor
- A trusted, organized friend

A short meeting today could save your family months of pain later.

Legacy in Real Life

Carla's mom had everything... somewhere. Insurance policies, bank statements, passwords; but no one knew where. It took Carla six months to locate accounts, claim benefits, and settle debts. "She meant well," Carla said. "She just didn't write it down or tell anyone. I won't do that to my kids."

Reflection & Application

- Does someone I trust know how to access my financial information?
- Have I reviewed and updated my beneficiary designations this year?
- Are my most important financial documents stored in one place?

Now take a step forward. Small actions can make an eternal difference.

- Create a secure binder or digital file for all key financial documents;
- Review and update beneficiary forms for insurance, retirement, and bank accounts;
- Schedule a "financial organization day" within the next month; and
- Invite someone you trust into your plan. Walk them through what you've prepared.

Declare this over yourself:

"I am a faithful steward. I prepare in wisdom. I plan in peace. I will not leave behind chaos. I will leave behind order, not confusion. I will leave a trail of peace."

End of Chapter Summary

Spiritual Principles

- **1 Corinthians 14:40** – Order reflects God's nature. Let your financial life reflect the same.
- **Proverbs 21:5** – Diligent planning leads to peace and provision.

- **Genesis 41:34–36** – Joseph's planning saved generations. Your preparation can preserve your family.

Theological Insights

- Finances are sacred because they touch the people God has entrusted to you.
- Clarity is a legacy. Order is a gift.
- You may not be able to take your wealth with you, but you can leave peace behind.
- God is not a God of confusion. Your paperwork shouldn't be either.

Your "business" should bless, not burden. Preparing your finances now is an act of spiritual maturity and a legacy of love.

Chapter 6: Updating What Matters

How to Keep Your Plans Current Through Life's Changes

Legacy from Scripture

King Hezekiah was told, *"Set your affairs in order, for you are going to die"* (2 Kings 20:1, NLT). He prayed, and God extended his life, but the command remained. **Our seasons change. So should our plans. Don't wait to get your house in order.**

If life teaches us anything, it's this: **seasons change**.

People change. Circumstances change. Relationships shift. New jobs, relocations, births, losses, divorces; life is in constant motion.

Yet, many treat their estate plans like a one-time task, written once and never revisited.

But here's the truth: even the best-drafted will becomes outdated if it no longer reflects your current relationships, responsibilities, and values.

"For everything there is a season, a time for every activity under heaven" (Ecclesiastes 3:1, NLT). That includes a time to update what matters.

Imagine this: years ago, you named your sister as your executor. Today, the relationship is distant. She lives in another state. You barely talk. But your legal documents still say she's in charge.

Now imagine a crisis. That outdated decision becomes today's problem, creating unnecessary strain for your family. And it's completely avoidable.

God says in Isaiah 43:19, *"See, I am doing a new thing! Now it springs up; do you not perceive it?"* God is always moving. And when He shifts our lives, our stewardship must shift with Him.

To ignore that movement is to let your past direct your future.

Updating your plans isn't just paperwork; it's worship. It says, "Lord, I see what You're doing, and I'm aligning every area of my life with it."

Estate planning is not a one-and-done task. It's a living discipline. As life changes, your plans should too.

1. Update Your Will

Your will should reflect your current relationships, property, and spiritual priorities.

Update your will if:

- You've had a birth, death, marriage, divorce, or adoption;
- You want to change your beneficiaries or executor;
- You've acquired or sold significant property; or
- Your values or intentions have changed.

Don't assume it's "close enough." Legal clarity matters. A small oversight could create big confusion.

2. Review Powers of Attorney

Your Medical Power of Attorney (MPOA) and Durable Power of Attorney (DPOA) should reflect who you trust today, not five years ago.

Update if:

- The person you named is no longer appropriate or available;

- You've developed a deeper relationship with someone more aligned with your values; or
- Your wishes or comfort with end-of-life decisions have changed.

These roles are sacred. Choose people who will honor your life and your faith, not just people who are convenient.

3. Recheck Beneficiary Designations

Many people don't realize this: **your beneficiary forms override your will.**

This includes:

- Life insurance
- Retirement accounts (401(k), IRA)
- Payable-on-Death (POD) bank accounts

Update these if:

- You've experienced a marriage, divorce, birth, or death;
- You want to remove someone or add a new loved one; or
- You notice discrepancies between your will and your account forms.

A mistake here can cost your loved ones dearly.

4. Review Funeral Instructions

You may have already chosen burial or cremation and selected hymns or Scriptures, but:

- Are your preferences still the same?
- Are they documented clearly and easy to find?
- Have you prepaid or made a preneed agreement?
- Do your loved ones know your wishes?

As your theology, relationships, or spiritual priorities evolve, so might your desire for how your life should be remembered.

5. Communicate the Changes

Even if your documents are flawless, silence can still create confusion.

Update and inform:

- Your executor;
- Your medical and financial agents;
- Your spouse or adult children; and
- Your attorney or financial advisor.

A simple five-minute conversation can prevent a five-month ordeal.

Keeping your affairs in order should become a spiritual rhythm, one that reflects your life today, not just your past.

- **Annually** – Choose a consistent month (e.g., your birthday or a holiday) to check in;
- **After Major Life Events** – Marriage, birth, divorce, relocation, illness, or death; and
- **Every 3–5 Years** – Even if nothing dramatic has changed.

Let your planning reflect your current reality, not your past assumptions.

Legacy in Real Life

James remarried but never updated his will. When he passed, everything went to his ex-wife. His new wife of 7 years was left with nothing. The probate judge said, "The court must follow what's on paper, not what's assumed." Updating matters.

Reflection & Application

A legacy of clarity requires the courage to keep it current.

- What life changes have occurred that should be reflected in my documents?
- Am I holding on to outdated plans out of fear or procrastination?
- Who needs to be informed if I make an update?

Now take a step forward. Small actions can make an eternal difference.

- Schedule a yearly reminder to review your estate plan.
- Meet with an attorney or advisor if major changes have occurred.
- Create a checklist of your current legal documents with the last updated date.
- Communicate any changes to those named in your plan.

Declare this over yourself:

"I embrace God's new seasons and walk in wisdom. My plans reflect present obedience and future faith. I will not leave behind confusion. I will leave behind clarity. I will continually keep my house in order as an act of faith and love."

End of Chapter Summary

Spiritual Principles

- **Ecclesiastes 3:1** – Life changes. Stewardship requires attentiveness to each season.
- **Isaiah 43:19** – God is doing new things. Don't let old plans hinder new obedience.
- **Proverbs 27:23–24** – Know the condition of what's entrusted to you. Review and revise.

Theological Insights

- What was right in one season may need realignment in the next.
- Updating your plans is an act of spiritual maturity, not an administrative obligation.
- Neglected updates often become someone else's burden.
- Staying current honors God, protects your family, and reflects intentional love.

A living faith requires living stewardship. Don't let yesterday's decisions direct today's obedience.

Chapter 7: A Legacy That Speaks After You're Gone

Leaving More Than Things, Leaving Testimony and Peace

Legacy from Scripture

Abel, though dead, *"still speaks"* because of his faith (Hebrews 11:4, NLT). What you believe, say, and do today can echo long after you're gone.

Legacy isn't just what you leave in a bank; it's what you leave in people's hearts.

A true legacy doesn't begin after you die; it echoes from how you live.

Hebrews 11:4 (NLT) tells us, *"Although Abel is long dead, he still speaks to us by his example of faith."* Abel didn't leave a written will. He left a life that pleased God. His offering was accepted, his obedience remembered, and his testimony endured.

Your greatest legacy is not your possessions. It's your faith in action.

Jesus made it clear: the greatest commandments are to *"love the Lord your God with all your heart"* and *"love your neighbor as yourself"* (Matthew 22:37–39, NLT). These are not suggestions. They are the foundation of a life that speaks beyond the grave.

- Did you live as salt, preserving what is holy and adding godly influence? (Matthew 5:13, NLT)
- Did your light shine, leading others to glorify God? (Matthew 5:14–16, NLT)
- Did your actions mirror compassion and conviction? (1 John 3:18, NLT; James 2:17, NLT)

James 1:27 (NLT) reminds us that *"pure and genuine religion"* is to care for orphans and widows. That's not ceremonial faith; it's sacrificial love.

Your real legacy may not be in your bank account, but in the burdens you lifted, the mercy you extended, the prayers you whispered, and the example you set.

So ask yourself:

- Will your children or spiritual heirs know what mattered to you?
- Will your testimony outlive your timeline?

If you want to leave a legacy that matters in heaven, don't just document your desires; **live your devotion**.

Let's get practical about how to preserve a spiritual legacy, not just an estate.

1. Legacy Letters & Video Messages

Use a legacy letter or video to speak directly to your loved ones. Share:

- Your faith testimony;
- Prayers and Scriptures that sustained you;
- Life lessons, especially those born out of failure, surrender, or transformation; and
- Your hopes and blessings for the next generation.

Let your voice remind them of God's love. Let your story inspire theirs.

2. Ethical Wills

An ethical will is a document that expresses your values, beliefs, and life principles. Unlike a legal will, it passes on what guided your heart.

Include:

- The Scriptures and convictions you stood on;
- The causes and ministries you supported;
- The people you forgave; and
- The reasons behind your decisions.

This is where you invite your family not just to remember you, but to follow you as you followed Christ (1 Corinthians 11:1, NLT).

3. Faith in Action (Spiritual Resume)

Legacy isn't what you say; it's what they saw.

Make a list that reflects your lived-out faith:

- Disciples you mentored;
- Ministries you served;
- Mission trips or outreach you supported;
- Prayers you offered for others; and

- Sacrifices you made in obedience to God.

Your legacy is built in the secret places, where obedience lived louder than applause.

4. Funeral & Memorial Planning

Your funeral or memorial service is the final platform for your witness.

You can:

- Choose Scriptures and songs that point people to Christ;
- Select who will speak or officiate;
- Specify the tone: celebration, worship, altar call; or
- Request donations be made to ministries or causes close to your heart.

Let your memorial declare the gospel.

Planning ahead protects your family from guessing and honors God with clarity.

5. Charitable Giving as Legacy

Your legacy can extend beyond your family to bless the Kingdom of God.

Scripture says:

- *"Honor the Lord with your wealth..."* (Proverbs 3:9, NLT)
- *"If you help the poor, you are lending to the LORD..."* (Proverbs 19:17, NLT)
- *"You must each decide in your heart how much to give..."* (2 Corinthians 9:7, NLT)

Ways to give charitably through your estate:

- Leave a percentage of your estate to a church, ministry, or nonprofit;
- Make a charitable organization a beneficiary of a retirement or insurance account;
- Fund a scholarship, mission, or outreach initiative; or
- Establish a donor-advised fund or trust.

This kind of giving multiplies your impact and honors God long after you're gone.

Legacy in Real Life

At her mother's funeral, Denise read a letter her mom had written. It was full of Scripture, forgiveness, and encouragement. There wasn't a dry eye in the room.

"That letter," Denise said, "was her real legacy. It gave me strength. I hear her voice every time I read it."

Reflection & Application

The most powerful legacy isn't what you leave behind, it's what you pass on.

- Am I living a life that glorifies God and loves others?
- Would my children or spiritual heirs know my testimony if all they had were my words?
- Have I taken intentional steps to leave behind more than possessions?

Now take a step forward. Small actions can make an eternal difference.

- Begin or update your ethical will: include Scripture, values, and life lessons.
- Write a legacy letter or record a short message for your family.
- Plan your funeral or memorial with the gospel in mind.
- Identify a ministry or mission to support through charitable giving.

Declare this over yourself:

"My legacy is a life surrendered to Christ. I will love God, love others, and leave a trail of truth behind me. My voice will not die with me. I will speak through love, faith, and wisdom passed on to those I leave behind."

End of Chapter Summary

Spiritual Principles

- **Hebrews 11:4** – A life of faith speaks even after death.
- **Proverbs 20:7** – A righteous life blesses generations.
- **Deuteronomy 6:6–7** – God's truth must be modeled and taught intentionally.
- **Matthew 22:37–39** – Legacy is built on loving God and others.
- **Matthew 5:13–16** – Be salt and light, publicly and boldly.
- **James 1:27** – Compassion is central to our spiritual inheritance.
- **Matthew 25:40** – Eternal legacy is built through earthly service.

Theological Insights

- Legacy is not about applause: it's about obedience.
- The greatest thing you can leave behind is evidence that Christ lived in you.
- The Book of Acts is still being written; your story matters.
- Charitable giving is a form of eternal investment.

The best parts of your life shouldn't be buried with you. Let your faith live on through your words, your works, and your worship.

Chapter 8: Final Checklist

Spiritual and Natural Tools to Use Right Now

Legacy from Scripture

Paul, near the end of his life, said: ***"I have fought the good fight, I have finished the race, and I have remained faithful"*** (2 Timothy 4:7, NLT).

That's the goal—not just to die, but to finish well, with your faith intact and your house in order.

Preparation is not a sign of fear; it's a sign of faith.

We don't prepare because we expect to die tomorrow. We prepare because we expect to meet God; and we want to do so with our house in order.

Like Paul, we want to be able to say at the end of our lives that we have fought faithfully, finished the race, and kept the faith.

That kind of confidence doesn't come from guesswork. It comes from stewardship.

To finish well is to finish with clarity. To finish with peace. To finish with nothing undone.

"So, dear brothers and sisters, work hard to prove that you really are among those God has called and chosen" (2 Peter 1:10, NLT).

Your eternal preparation is the highest priority. But earthly preparation (done with love and wisdom) is part of your spiritual legacy.

Imagine the peace of knowing your family won't be left scrambling, guessing, or second-guessing. That's not just good planning; that's spiritual maturity. It's mercy in motion.

This chapter is your final roadmap: a spiritual and natural checklist designed to walk you through what faithful preparation really looks like.

This checklist gathers everything you've learned—faith, planning, stewardship, and testimony—into a single, clear list. You don't need to do everything in one day, but you do need to begin.

The Essentials Checklist

Spiritual Preparation

- I have accepted Christ and confirmed my salvation.
- I have shared my testimony with loved ones.
- I have considered how my funeral or memorial will point to Jesus.

Legal Documents

- Last Will and Testament is created, signed, and stored.
- The Executor has been named and informed.
- Medical Power of Attorney is assigned.
- Financial Power of Attorney is assigned.
- Living Will/Advance Directive is completed.
- HIPAA Authorization is signed.
- Guardianship documents are in place (if applicable).

Financial Affairs

- Beneficiaries are updated on all accounts (retirement, insurance, POD).
- Account details and access instructions are documented.

- Passwords and digital assets are stored securely.
- Final expense or burial insurance has been reviewed.
- Debts, mortgages, and liabilities are clearly listed.

Final Wishes

- Funeral instructions are written and shared.
- Burial or cremation preferences are documented.
- Obituary preferences (optional) are outlined.
- Charitable giving plans are included in the estate or will.
- Memorial preferences reflect gospel-centered values.

Communication & Storage

- All key documents are stored securely and accessible.
- A trusted person knows where everything is.
- The executor and agents have been briefed on their roles.

Review & Readiness Routine

Planning isn't a one-time task. It's a rhythm of faithful stewardship.

- I have scheduled an **annual estate review** (e.g., every birthday or New Year).
- I know to update my plan after **major life events**:
  - Births
  - Deaths
  - Marriages
  - Divorces
  - Relocations
  - Medical Diagnoses
  - Changes in dependents or caregiving responsibilities
- I've considered holding a **family readiness meeting** to review what I've prepared.

Legacy in Real Life

One of my clients kept a simple binder on a shelf. After she passed, her daughter said, "Everything we needed was in that folder. It was sad, but it was peaceful. She gave us the gift of order."

Death didn't bring confusion. It brought closure.

Reflection & Application

Preparation is love in action—finish what you started.

- Have I completed the steps I've learned throughout this book?
- Which areas still need my attention?
- Who do I need to inform about what I've prepared?

Now take a step forward. Small actions can make an eternal difference.

- Download or print this checklist and keep it in your estate binder; and
- Schedule a conversation with your executor or adult children.

Share this book with someone you love. Help them get their house in order too.

Declare this over yourself:

> "I have fought the good fight. I have finished my race. I have kept the faith; and I leave nothing undone. I have prepared with purpose. I walk in peace, knowing I've stewarded what God entrusted to me. My life speaks, and my

legacy reflects the order, love, and truth of God."

End of Chapter Summary

Spiritual Principles

- **2 Peter 1:10** – Confirm your calling with intentional effort.
- **1 Corinthians 9:24** – Run your race with intention, not delay.
- **2 Timothy 4:7** – A faithful life finishes with peace and purpose.

Theological Insights

- God's people finish well with order, not confusion.
- Faith and planning are not at odds; they are partners.
- Final preparation is not about fear; it's about readiness.
- The Gospel is not only preached in pulpits. It's declared in how we live, and how we leave.

Preparing for your death is an act of devotion. It says to your family, *"I loved you enough to make this easier."*

It says to God, *"I trusted You enough to get my house in order."*

Final Word: Leave Nothing Undone

A Personal Message from My Heart to Yours

If you've made it this far, thank you.

Thank you for leaning into the hard work of preparation, for facing what most people avoid, for praying through difficult truths, and for taking bold steps. Whether you've completed every task in this book or are just beginning, you are walking in wisdom, and God honors that.

The world may still encourage delay or denial. But you are different. You are a person of faith and order, a person who prepares not out of fear but out of love and obedience.

As we close, I want to remind you of this:
God is not the author of confusion. He is the God of clarity, peace, and completion.

Jesus said, ***"It is finished"*** (John 19:30, NLT). That wasn't just about His mission; it's our example. When your time comes, whether near or far, my prayer is that you too can echo those words, knowing you didn't leave behind fear, debt, or confusion but testimony, preparation, and peace.

You've written your wishes, you've organized your documents, but more importantly, you've aligned your heart with eternity. That matters more than anything you could leave in a binder or a bank account.

If your loved ones are reading this after your passing, let these words be for them too:
You were loved.
You were prepared for this.
You were not left alone in the storm.

If you're still holding back on something, start now.
If you've checked all the boxes, stay ready.
If you've accepted Christ through this journey, welcome home.

This may be the last chapter, but it's not the end of your impact.

Live well. Love well. Leave nothing undone.

With love and deep gratitude,

B. Faye Anderson

Appendix

Final Checklist – Get Your Death in Order

- I have written and signed a last will and testament.
- My executor has been chosen and informed of their responsibilities.
- I've created or updated my medical power of attorney and living will.
- My durable power of attorney for finances is in place.
- My funeral and burial preferences are written down and shared.
- All beneficiary designations on accounts are current.
- A secure folder or binder contains all critical documents.
- I've shared the location of documents with a trusted person.
- I've written a legacy letter or recorded a message for my loved ones.
- I've reviewed and updated my plan within the last 12 months.
- I have accepted Christ and am confident in my eternal preparation.

Templates and Tools for Getting Your House in Order

These sample templates are not intended as legal advice or substitutes for state-specific legal documents. They are simply meant to help you organize your thoughts and begin important conversations with your family and advisors.

Important Note: Before relying on any template, consult an attorney in your state or jurisdiction to ensure compliance with applicable laws.

Letter of Instruction

This is a nonlegal, informal document to help your family know where things are and what to do. It can be stored with your estate planning documents.

Sample Letter of Instruction

Dear [Family Member / Executor / Loved One's Name],

If you are reading this, I've gone home to be with the Lord.

First, know that I love you. My hope is that this letter brings clarity, peace, and a sense of preparation in the days ahead.

Please find all of my important documents in [location, e.g., a binder in the safe / a folder labeled "Estate Plan" in my office / online vault with password].

Here are key things you'll need:

• A copy of my will and any trusts;
• My birth certificate, social security card, driver's license, and marriage license (if applicable);

- Account information (bank, retirement, insurance);
- Funeral and burial preferences;
- Contact list for my attorney, financial advisor, and pastor; and
- Any prepaid plans or outstanding debts.

If I haven't already told you: Thank you. Thank you for loving me, helping me, and honoring my wishes.

My greatest prayer is that you'll walk closely with God, love each other well, and find peace in knowing I am with Him.

With love,
[Your Name]
[Date]

Legacy Letter

A legacy letter is a spiritual message to loved ones that shares your values, faith, and blessings. It's not about logistics; it's about heart.

Sample Legacy Letter

To my children and grandchildren,

If I could leave you one thing, it wouldn't be a house or money. It would be faith. The kind that held me when life fell apart. The kind that kept me going when I was weary. The kind that led me to Jesus.

I want you to know that I prayed for you, even before you were born. I prayed that you would be kind, wise, and anchored in truth. I prayed that you would love God deeply and love others fiercely.

Remember that success is not measured in status, but in obedience. Stay humble. Serve well. And don't ever think you have to be perfect to be loved by God or by me.

Love, [Your Name]

End-of-Life Information Worksheet

Use this worksheet to keep vital information in one place. You can customize it or keep a digital copy that you update annually or as needed.

Category	Details
Full Legal Name	
Date of Birth	
Social Security Number	
Current Address	
Health Insurance Provider	

Primary Care Physician	
Specialist Medical Providers	
Medications/Allergies	
Life Insurance Policies *Company, Contact Info, Policy Number*	
Retirement Accounts *Institution(s), Account Number(s),* *Beneficiary(ies)*	
Bank Accounts *Institution, Account Type, Routing* *Number, Account Number, POD* *Instructions*	

Safe Deposit Box *Institution, Location, Keyholder(s)*	
Funeral Preferences *Preferences (burial/cremation), Service Location, Clergy*	
Obituary Details *Who should be notified?*	
Charities to Support *Name(s) and instructions*	
Digital Accounts & Passwords *Location of master password and other passwords*	**Do not list here.**

Scripture Suggestions for Funeral or Memorial Services

You may want to include your favorite Scriptures or select verses for a memorial service that reflect your faith and offer comfort to your loved ones.

Suggested Scriptures:

- Psalm 23 (NLT): *"The Lord is my shepherd..."*
- John 14:1–3(NLT): *"Don't let your hearts be troubled..."*
- 1 Thessalonians 4:13–18 (NLT): *The Hope of the Resurrection*
- 2 Timothy 4:7 (NLT): *"I have fought the good fight..."*
- Romans 8:38–39 (NLT): *"And I am convinced that nothing can ever separate us from God's love..."*

Songs or Hymns for Funeral or Worship

Include your preferred selections. Choose songs that reflect your relationship with God and your hope in eternity.

Examples:

- *It Is Well with My Soul*
- *Total Praise*
- *I'll Fly Away*
- *Great Is Thy Faithfulness*
- *Because He Lives*

A Note to You

As you create your estate planning documents, remember:

- **Select wisely.** Choose executors, agents under your Power of Attorney, and medical decision-makers who are trustworthy and capable.

- **Confirm willingness.** Talk with each person you've named to ensure they are ready, willing, and able to serve in their role.

- **Communicate clearly.** Let them know what responsibilities may be involved, and answer any questions they have.

- **Provide access.** Give them copies of the documents, or at least tell them exactly where the originals are stored.

- **Stay current.** Revisit these choices over time to make sure your documents and your team of helpers still reflect your wishes.

Final Encouragement

This appendix is not the end of your journey. It is the beginning of a life lived in readiness. Revisit it each year and update it to account for life's changes. Share your plan with those you trust to carry out your wishes. And share this book and these insights with those you believe it may serve.

Let your planning be an act of worship so that you leave a legacy that is a reflection of God's order, peace, and love.

About the Author

B. Faye Anderson, Esq. is an attorney and pastor who helps individuals and families prepare for both life and legacy. With over 15 years of experience in corporate and Christian leadership, she brings a blend of practical knowledge and spiritual clarity to every conversation about purpose, preparation, and faith.

B. Faye Anderson is passionate about equipping others with the knowledge and tools to protect their families, steward their legacy with confidence, and ultimately walk with God in a way that leads them to see Him face-to-face. As a youth pastor and speaker, she is known for heart-centered, truth-driven teaching that empowers believers to live with intention.

A devoted wife and mother of two, B. Faye Anderson believes in leaving nothing undone legally, spiritually, or relationally.

To learn more about B. Faye Anderson's ministry and find resources for faith, family, and legacy, visit www.anchoredlifepublishing.com.